The Gardens of Flora Baum

I

The Gardens of Flora Baum

Book One: By the Tree of Life
  Part 1   Sum
  Part 2   The Path Approaching
  Part 3   Epiphany
  Part 4   The Waves Receding
  Part 5   Difference

Book Two: Towards a Greek Garden
  Part 1   The Program
  Part 2   Iliad
  Part 3   The History
  Part 4   Odyssey
  Part 5   The Diagram

Book Three: Rome
  Part 1   Urbiculture
  Part 2   Floralia
  Part 3   Umbrageous Vision

Book Four: Towards Farthest Thule
  Part 1   Lay of the Last Monk
  Part 2   Sibyl
  Part 3   Lyre, Harp, Violin

Book Five: By the Tree of Knowledge
  Part 1   By the Tree
  Part 2   The Tree of Knowledge
  Part 3   Knowledge
  Part 4   Of Knowledge by the Tree
  Part 5   Tree
  Part 6   Knowledge of the Tree
  Part 7   Of the Tree

BOOKS	PARTS	PARTS
Book One	5	
		10
Book Two	5	
Book Three	3	3
Book Four	3	
		10
Book Five	7	

The Gardens of Flora Baum

◆

Book One

By the Tree of Life

Julia Budenz

Carpathia Press
Chelmsford, Mass., U.S.A.

Carpathia Press
7 Colonial Terrace
Chelmsford, Massachusetts 01824
U.S.A.

© 2011 by the Estate of Julia Budenz
All rights reserved.

Published by Carpathia Press. Except for brief passages quoted in a review, no part of this book may be reproduced by any mechanical, photographic, or electronic process without the written permission of the Estate of Julia Budenz. Address such requests to Carpathia Press, 7 Colonial Terrace, Chelmsford, MA 01824. Printed in the United States of America.

Library of Congress Cataloging-in-Publication Data has been applied for.

ISBN: 978-0-9849089-1-2 (softcover, bk. 1)

GOD *Almightie* first Planted a *Garden*.

Francis Bacon.

Vulgus resistentiam quiescentibus & impetum moventibus tribuit: sed motus & quies, uti vulgo concipiuntur, respectu solo distinguuntur ab invicem. . . .

Isaac Newton.

Foreword

THIS IS A posthumous publication, but Julia Budenz had meticulously prepared her five-book poem and had overseen the process of digitization and proofing, and so it has the stamp of authorial approval. It rests on the author's typed version. Only the few pieces written within a week of her death on December 11, 2010, are from manuscript, and these are inserted at the points she indicated. They are "September" and "And January" (Book Three, pages 718–720, 722) and "How shall I say this?" (Book Five, page 570).

Her long poem addresses a wide range of readers, and she would have wished this first contact to be an unmediated one. So no attempt is made here to categorize, other than to indicate, as the poet did herself, that there is a different focus in each of the five books. In a short essay called "Query Re One's Work," which appeared online in the *Poetry Porch* in 1997, she said:

> The gardens are five, comprising the five books. The first garden is the garden of the holy; its book explores transcendence, is located partially in Eden, and draws upon imagery from the Bible and the liturgy. Its title, "By the Tree of Life," indicates that despite its strong center this book may be considered a Paradise Lost, as is suggested also by the names of its five parts: "Sum," "The Path Approaching," "Epiphany," "The Waves Receding," and "Difference."
>
> The second garden is the garden of the beautiful; its book contemplates the aesthetic, is situated partially in Greece, and makes use of Greek literature, mythology, and geography. This second book, which is called "Towards a Greek Garden," has a midpoint as well as a final destination and also consists of five parts, whose names intimate both the patterned centering and the linear progression: "The Program," "Iliad," "The History," "Odyssey," "The Diagram." Since Flora Baum reaches the Greek garden, the second book may be designated a Paradise Regained.
>
> The third garden is that of the true, specifically of academic

knowledge, of scholarship, of learning. Its book, entitled "Rome," uses material from Roman literature, history, and topography. This is the pivotal book in the design and development of the poem; its three parts — "Urbiculture," "Floralia," and "Umbrageous Vision" — mark not only a center which is both city and garden but also a difficult struggle to pass through pedantry to erudition and insight.

The fourth garden is that of the good and blooms with human relations. Its book, "Towards Farthest Thule," is set partly in Britain, finally in Shetland. As might be expected, it utilizes English and Scottish literature, folklore, and geography. The book begins with a long ballad, "The Lay of the Last Monk," continues with an epyllion called "Sibyl," and concludes with a sequence of lyrics, "Lyre, Harp, Violin."

The fifth and final garden is the garden of the whole. Its book, "By the Tree of Knowledge," is the philosophical book, the one most fully placed in Flora's native America but also situated in her native world, in her homeland the earth, in her home the universe. It is the book of the elm, rooted and reaching. It grounds itself not only in a meditation upon philosophy but also in social science and physical science, in culture and nature, in the microcosm and the mesocosm and the macrocosm, in the final paracosm, the final paradigm and paradise. It is the book which I will write if I can live long enough and become wise enough to do it. "O mihi tum longae maneat pars ultima vitae," I find myself crying out with Virgil, hoping to touch this great beginning or end or center or edge.

Although no critical assessment is offered here, it can be anticipated that, in due course, *The Gardens of Flora Baum* will find a place in the history of American literature once readers have had a chance to absorb its author's new and distinctive voice and to respond fully to it.

Julia's life and writing were intertwined and the following biographical sketch may prove helpful. She was the eldest daughter of Louis Budenz and Margaret Rodgers Budenz and had three sisters. She was born on May 23, 1934, in New York City. The first break in her life came in 1945 when her father renounced the Communist party and rejoined the Roman Catholic church. The family moved briefly to South Bend, Indiana, before returning to New York. The year 1956 marked Julia's graduation with an A.B. summa cum laude from the College of New Rochelle and also the beginning of the period she spent as an Ursuline nun. In 1962, she was awarded a Master of Arts degree at Catholic University and became an instructor in classics at the College of New Rochelle.

In 1966, after leaving the convent, she studied briefly at New York University in the spring and began graduate studies in comparative literature (Greek, Latin and English) at Harvard University in the fall. She graduated A.M. in 1972 and continued working towards a Ph.D. for a time, but the pull of scholarship in isolation became less compelling than the desire to create in the light of her scholarship and her vision. She began writing *The Gardens of Flora Baum* in about 1969 and received a fellowship at the Radcliffe Institute in 1974–75 for the purpose of developing it.

For the rest of her working life, she undertook paid employment with an eye always to the opportunities offered for the combination of scholarly facilities and leisure essential for her writing. Widener Library at Harvard University had the central place in her life that she speaks of in her poem. In 1972, she had begun working in Harvard's History of Science Department with I. Bernard Cohen and Anne Whitman on their new English translation of Isaac Newton's *Principia*, and, although she left Cambridge twice to teach classics — at Colby College in 1980–81 and at Berea College in 1987–88 — she was mainly engaged on History of Science Department projects until her retirement freed her to concentrate on her poetry. She suffered from ill health in her closing years and died of cancer at the age of seventy-six.

Parts of *The Gardens of Flora Baum* have been published previously in books and periodicals. *From the Gardens of Flora Baum*, Wesleyan University Press, Middletown, Connecticut, 1984, contained "The Fire Escape" and "The Sheen" (Book Two, pages 173–250), and *Carmina Carmentis*, Pivot Press, Brooklyn, New York, 2005, contained a sequence from "January" (Book Three, pages 635–673). Shorter pieces from *The Gardens of Flora Baum* were included in these edited books: *Anthology of Magazine Verse and Yearbook of American Poetry*, ed. Alan F. Pater, Monitor Book Company, Beverly Hills, California, 1980; *A Formal Feeling Comes: Poems in Form by Contemporary Women*, ed. Annie Finch, Story Line

Press, Brownsville, Oregon, 1994; *Catullus in English*, ed. Julia Haig Gaisser, Penguin Books, London, 2001; *Emily Lyle: The Persistent Scholar*, ed. Frances J. Fischer and Sigrid Rieuwerts, WVT Wissenschaftlicher Verlag Trier, Trier, 2007; *Petrarch & Dante*, ed. Zygmunt G. Baranski and Theodore J. Cachey, Jr., University of Notre Dame Press, Notre Dame, Indiana, 2009.

Other excerpts from the work appeared between 1971 and 2010 in the following periodicals: *Akros, American Arts Quarterly, The American Voice, Amphora, Arion, Bits, Bitterroot, Boston Review, Bunting Institute Newsletter, Chapman, Cloelia, Cosmos, Crazyhorse, The Cream City Review, Cross Currents, Epos, Four Quarters, La Fusta, Harvard Advocate, Harvard Review, Italian Americana, The Kenyon Review, Lines Review, The Lyric, Mati, NEeuropa, New England Classical Journal, North Stone Review, Notre Dame Review, Other Poetry, Persephone, Poet Lore, The Poetry Porch, Radcliffe Quarterly, Rhino, Scottish Literary Journal, Society of Fellows News* (American Academy in Rome), *The Society of Institute Fellows Newsletter* (The Bunting Institute of Radcliffe College), *Southwest Review, Sparrow, Studia Mystica, The Tennessee Quarterly, The Tennessee Review, Vergilius, The Wallace Stevens Journal, William and Mary Review*, and *YIP: Yale Italian Poetry*.

Very warm acknowledgement should be made in conclusion to those bodies that, through residencies, fellowships, visiting scholar appointments, and funding, gave support to this long-term poetic project. I shall instance with gratitude the American Academy in Rome, the Authors League, the Bellagio Study and Conference Center of the Rockefeller Foundation, the Djerassi Foundation, Harvard University's Departments of Comparative Literature and English, the National Endowment for the Arts, the Radcliffe Institute, and Yaddo.

EMILY LYLE
University of Edinburgh

Publisher's Note

WHEN JULIA BUDENZ began writing *The Gardens of Flora Baum* in about 1969, she prepared master sheets on a manual typewriter. By 2005 she had switched to a laptop computer, which provided digital files. The arduous task of scanning the older material (roughly 1,700 pages), processing it with optical-character-recognition software, and proofreading it was overseen by Emily Lyle. For questions that arise, readers should consult the original typescript included among Julia's papers, which have been placed on deposit in the Houghton Library, Harvard University.

Over the years Julia told friends the schedule she'd mapped out for herself, intending to finish *The Gardens of Flora Baum* in 2015, when she would have been 81. But in January 2008 she asked me to explore the idea of an "introductory edition" of the material written to that point, much of which had not yet appeared in print. She continued work on unfinished sections, mainly in Book Four and Book Five. By late 2010, with her health in sharp decline, she identified those places in the poem where she'd intended to insert further material.

In the last few months of her life she did make sure that the start and finish of every book were completed. She also discussed her preferences as to the layout and presentation of the books.

Layout and style. In preparing this set of five books for publication, my aim has been to follow the original typescript to the greatest extent possible. In most cases short titled pieces begin on a new page, or are run on with preceding pieces. The decision whether to center a title or place it flush left also follows the original. But a typewriter does not offer the stylistic variation possible in a typeset book, and we have varied heading styles to suggest the importance of each piece in the hierarchy implied by the table of contents of each book. The scheme varies somewhat from book to book.

The author's practice of having complete stanzas on a page, whenever possible, explains why some pages end short even though the piece continues on the next page. In the case of very long stanzas and other layout problems, we occasionally did break stanzas. This is indicated by the quaint device of a "catchword," set flush right at the bottom of the page. The catchword repeats the first word or two on the next page and tells the reader that the stanza has not ended yet. (To prevent anyone from mistaking a catchword for the second part of a broken line in the poem's meter, the catchword is printed in smaller type.) No catchwords were needed in Book One, but they do occur often in later books. On pages without a catchword, the page does end in a stanza break.

Occasionally the poem contains insertions that may appear to have been added by someone other than the author. One example is the use of "[sic]" in two places on page 79 of Book Two. Another is the inclusion of several footnotes in Book Five about a missing word or illegible date in a personal letter. There are a few other cases of partially bracketed dates at the tops of personal letters. All these insertions were made by Julia Budenz herself; she clearly intended them to be considered part of her poem.

Three asterisks (* * *) centered on a line denote a *lacuna*, or gap, where Julia had intended to write more material. On several occasions she commented that the asterisks could represent one stanza, one piece, or a long section of many pieces — there's no telling.

But the poem in five books appears to be at least 90 percent finished to her satisfaction. For the record, it contains about 303,700 words in 2,254 printed pages. The original typescript has 2,282 pages (owing to some differences in the locations of page breaks).

For advice and suggestions on specific issues during the preparation of these volumes, I am grateful to Virginia Furtwangler, Rebecca and Douglas Karo, Hope Mayo, Arthur Mortensen, Cynthia Thompson, and Frederick Turner. Without the monumental effort of Emily Lyle over many years, including repeated proofreading at various stages of production, this edition would not have been possible.

ROGER W. SINNOTT
Carpathia Press

Contents

Foreword   v
Publisher's Note   xi

Book One: By the Tree of Life

Part One: Sum   3

  Witness   5
  Heuristic   6
  I Can Rarely Remember   7

Part Two: The Path Approaching   9

  Crockery   11
  A Photograph   12
  Fourfold Purple   13
  Direction   14
  Lines   15
  Allegory   16
  From the Well   17
  A Spring   18
  Clearing   19
  Encounter   20
  Watching   21
  Heaven   22
  One Tree   23
  The One Tree   24
  By the Tree of Life   25
  The End   26
  Statement   27

January 5	28
Version	29

Part Three: Epiphany   31

January 6, 1 a.m. (Watch on a Shoestring)	33
January 6, 5 a.m.	34
The Rite of the Call	35
The Candle	36
The Veil	39
The Ring	42
The Crown	45
The Banquet	48
January 6, 1 p.m.	51
January 6, 5 p.m. (Watch in a Pocket)	52

Part Four: The Waves Receding   53

Fraction	55
January 14	56
When He Went Away	57
Vaunt	58
Anima	59
Considerations	60
Criticism	61
Limitation	62
Adaptation	63
Asseveration	64
Exegesis	65
Touches	66
What Happened	67
Afterward	68
Anapneusis	69
Later	70
Sunday Morning	71
Recall	72
Affect and Effect	73
Sequel	74
Precision	75

Sequence	76
Effect and Cause	77
Consequence	78
Narcissus	79
Ingredients	80
I Won't Say Yet	81
Resume	82
Sloughing	84
Finding	85
Romulus Religiosulus	86
Lemma	87
It Was Nice	88
Comparing	89
We	90
Journal	91
Passage	92
Shaking	93
Unshaken	94
Your Right Hand	95
Advent	96
This Night	100
Fairy Tale	101
My Flower	102
Playground	103
Astronomia Nova	104
Muddy Reflection	105
Sidereus Nuncius	106
A Black Hole	111
Commemoration	112
Part Five: Difference	113
Sometimes It's Hard	115
Anamnestic	116
Pygmalion	117

Book One

By the Tree of Life

Part One

Sum

Witness

I don't ask you to believe what I have seen.
I don't believe it myself. I only see it,
And I tell you as a point of information.
There are some cracks in the world.
There are some windows in the sky.

I knew it when the luminous blood
Was pouring over a long October west
And fell into the oaks, down into the dogwoods,
Down, down along the euonymus rivers
And into the barberry brooks.

The sun has pricked a finger on a sprig of barberry,
And I have pricked my spirit on the sun.
There is a crack in my spirit,
There is a minimal window in my soul
Through which the sun that is not the sun thunders
And blood leaps like a geyser,

A crack through which the sun that is not the sun
Sucks up the blood that is the very blood
Surging in temples, a window
Through which I watch, past the galaxies,
What I cannot believe,
What I cannot tell.

Heuristic

She went back
To find, I guess, something.
She found it when she walked on the stone-paved path
Buttressed by chestnuts budding
In the wind of a morning in March.
The chestnuts were the ones that flung
Their fragrant lamps into the dusks of May
And arched the August afternoons.
The path was the kind of path
On which you walked not somewhere
But up and down. It was that same
Old path. She walked up and down.
Through thin shoes she felt the cut of the stone.
And she felt a self that she recognized as real,
A self that was a half,
One half, and the other
Is ideal.

I Can Rarely Remember

I can rarely remember now
Who it was that used to come
Into the stone building before dawn
Or after dusk, like a glowworm,
A pocket flashlight, a quarter moon
Waxing through the ticking of the dark
Into the encompassing quiet
Of a sun's bonfire.

Part Two

The Path Approaching

Crockery

Long lilies in a blue jug
Lean like swans
From a blue pond, like the long
Sweep of the sounding of violins
From a lake of tone, like souls
All straining from an azure globe,
Each from a blue-veined pot.

A Photograph

The wet light of azaleas set
Like lavender luminaries up
Against a wet green sky of leaf and lawn

Entered her camera. The film
When developed resembled the print
Of purple pansies near a bank

In the shopping center, or a view
Of wooden eyes wet with painted tears.
The sky was removed.

Fourfold Purple

But if the sky was removed then
She was out with the sky.
The big wet purple eye
Looked through the lashes of the elm
And the purple fingers of the crabapple in flower
At the purple fingers of the seaweed
And the hug of the purple ocean.

Direction

Or wasn't she really wearing
The weeds of the sea
As she beat the waves for a glimpse
Through breaks in cloud
Or rocked on the top in calms
With oculi wide?
Seas lie skyward.

Lines

The cosmos is mounted on feathers.
Fly away, bright flower.
Yet it is roots that lift us.
Down we go, seeking the top.
Out we reach, seeking the center.
In we tend, seeking the edges of being.
Nothingward we run, wanting all.

Allegory

The fourfold lilac flower has faced
The threefold rain. The first
Sprinkle of water

Rolled its little glistening beads
Down the sides of the lavender hollow.
Oily ambrosia

Slid more slowly, anointing the cup
Into gleam. The final fire
Was all of the sky.

From the Well

To describe that darkness and that desire
May be difficult, she thought. But they know
The long blindness before birth, the fumbling
Among the furniture of night, the sudden
Plunging down the pools of sleep,
And at the bottom the last press
Of the eyes, creating day-craving.

A Spring

Suspended pale-green torrents,
A pendulous pink fountain:
These were the sugar maples and the weeping cherry
At the end of that cold April.
She should have rejoiced, some said,
In sweet aqueous arrival
And the budding shower of the sun.
But she was chilled by the gigantic spray of shadow
Thrown from the gold streams of the big willow
That signified the infinite burning star.
Her tears were ice.

Clearing

The gray shores of the sky border
A widening pool of blue,
And while I look through
The order

Spinning in every circle made
By the cast of every glance,
The circles fade
And advance

And fade, throbbing the azure report
Of a thing of another sort
To correspond
Beyond.

Encounter

She sensed him as that day she sensed
The sudden sweetness of the locust
Spreading in late May air.

He rose more ethereal and strong
Than the ropy trunk of the locust
And the winy lightness of its leaves.

She walked there often to catch
A breath of limitless blossom
Or remembrance or white intimation.

Watching

There is an infinite sun nearby
At the end of a scope
To make it smaller, dimmer, manageable.
It's hard to manage
That infinite sun
Before my eyes,
Inside my breathing,
Here,
Other.

Heaven

I shall term it seeing
I shall name it light

We saw

We were plunged into white light
For ten thousand years
We saw the prisms of ourselves
And of our friends

And of the friends of our friends

We remembered the morning gold of the elm
In New England autumns
We remembered the burning bushes
Of October afternoons

They were as we remembered

And not dying
And the light was living and caressed us
And the next ten thousand years
We danced and we sang the light

And the next we saw and we saw

The light burned us like locust blossoms
We flamed like love
Like incense burning like spring
In luminous showers

We saw and we saw and we saw white light

We shall pass the term
We shall know the name

One Tree

One tree made a forest.
It was the fern-leaf beech
Arising, arising, into July, into noon;

A swirl of swifts twittered the hungry hour:
A cool salad, a chilly sip of lemonade,
Not this ambiguous edge of observation

In cloudless midday's pitilessness.
I stepped in below the green cumulation of cloud.
One tree made sweet evensong.

The One Tree

Yet seeing is all. I choose
To kneel in the sun and see.
Layer after layer the branches rise,

Their motion and stillness contained in my eyes.
Soon I am one with the tree,
The one tree, which I will not lose.

By the Tree of Life

In those days we ate beechnuts.
We walked in the garden at eventide.
And if there was something we did not know

We knew so much: the beginning and the end,
The way, the feel of the way,
The feel of the end.

The End

The end was endless: a green summer day
With wind in the leaves and shade on the grass
And white angels in the sky.

The sky was endless. We rested
In its blue. Its blue was not dust,
Not bordered by night. And though our hands

Bled from our climb and our knees
Were rough and our eyes were seared
And we never slept, we rested in the end.

Statement

This book is not like a poem. The form
And the content are not one. In fact,
I give you only the form
Of the feeling.

Flitting like a swift that is jerking over June
I can gulp the content — that is, a bit
Of the content, a fly as a speck
Of the atmosphere

That hovers above the settling green
Of June, the heavy leaves, the wet
Grass. The content is known
In unlikenesses.

January 5

I'll hold a candle tomorrow

Even if machine-age panes
Will amply guide the climbing day
Through stained-glass windows,
Even if electric bulbs
Will dangle, more than amber, strident,
From Gothic ceilings.

This is like a shore where nothing
Is awake, nothing is alive.
It's too early even for witchhazel
To spread those fresh and fragrant solicular
Rays over long-grayed snow.
But here from one amber globe
Four yellow strings are uncrumpling before their time. Before time
The sun for which this stranded wick
Shivers was burning. I can feel

Five fingers uncurl.

Version

For
Reaching for
If you
When you
Since you
Turn
Mark
Will
Turn
Translate into illumination

Part Three

Epiphany

January 6

1 a.m.

(*Watch on a Shoestring*)

Just let me live until morning. Her cell was black.
The white bed creaked as she turned once again and felt
The chilly floor for her watch. Too dark to check.
She lay with the black string dangling from a dangling hand.
Just let me live until morning, when time will end.

January 6

5 a.m.

Inhabitants issue from the meager bedrooms.
By the path some sun-yellow tentacles stretch
As the winter witchhazel feels for spring.
I know this from yesterday's ding-a-ling.
I am staring toward the doorway of the sun.

The Rite of the Call

The Candle

1.

In the cave of the night
A glimmer occurs
As of a star, as of a sun.

Daughter, awake with the moon.
Wise one, arise. The word is crying
From before the foundation of the world.

Dress in this dark, walk in this white,
Throwing aside the things of a child.
Seize the torch. And go

To meet the light as he rises upon your cold shore.
Behold him running as a giant in the east.
Behold his fire.

Wise one, follow that star.
Have you lit your lamp in the dawn?
Have you clasped the smooth, the columned wax

And lifted the flame to the rubescent sky?
Have you listened? Exult. He is coming.
Daughter, come. Bride, come. Come, mine.

With the sparkling of stars on the floor of the desert of snow
Lilac shadows edge
Footprints to the flickering sea.

2.

The wide, white moon is sliding out of the night
While over the ice the calling star of journey turns,
Is returning. The woman stirs on the desolate bed of the west.

I sleep, and my heart watches.
The voice of my beloved, behold he comes
This night, this hour.

This night is the black-bound book where the shimmering path is read.
This night is the glory over the door of rutilant blessing.
This night is day.

I shiver. The frigid light of the moon
Begins to glow as the light of the sun
And the light of the sun as the splendor of seven mornings.

Awake, yes, awake, O my soul, I will dress in the dawn.
Yes, arise, I will put on the sun.
I tremble. Yes. I will. I will don this day.

Your eyes are flames. And now
I come. And now I follow.
And now with all my heart I watch and listen and follow.

The taper plated with ice is alight with the rose-gold word.
The beholder is clothed in the flowing of white as she strides
Grasping the shaft of the pillaring fire.

3.

She kneels in night on the gelid desert, the algid shore.
She bends her head in the dazzle
Of daying. She bows before the blaze.

Take me according to your word, great word;
At your name the winter will melt. I shall live.
At the last I shall pass to the land where the lamp is the lamb.

Radiance, have mercy now.
Brightness, have mercy now.
Radiance, have mercy now.

All who have been, pray for us.
All who are now, pray for us.
All who will be, pray for us.

Brightness, who began the dawn,
Accomplish the day,
And be her sheen, her clarity, her empyrean.

Stand as a lantern before my eyes.
Gleam as a standard before my feet.
Bear me, unbearable fire.

Prostrate and silent she lies on the glimmering floor of the cavern,
Yearning while slowly the tenebrous remnants of conglaciation
Feel hot rays.

The Veil

1.

After the sought long dawning the glare on the sand of the morning
Stays by the sea. And a blackening cloud shades, veils with its mercy
Only the chosen who chooses. A voice in the thunder is calling.

Come. Plunge. Go under. Leave your land
And enter the land I will show you. Bathe as a bride
Through the word in the rain. Seek birth by water.

Listen. As in the beginning, like a wind,
I will breathe on the sea, and the sea
Will part and the river will turn. I will move

Over the waters and through the dark
Of the deep. I come in cloud
To cover you now. I will lead you through

The flood. I will make a way,
And the sea is a way, and the walls of water
Build. I will go before you.

Come, my chosen, and I will pose
In you my throne. For the king desires your beauty, your black
Obnubilation. Take my veil.

From over the melting shreds of the lenten snow
And deepening puddles and mud, from the nebulous heaven,
A hidden mornly moon calls to the sea.

2.

Where she had wept in the desert and where she had known no shelter,
Where she had sat on the bank, by the yellower willows she listens,
Lifting her arms to the mist as it falls.

Dread darkness, in you I will go through oceans.
A voice is over the waters, over the many waters
A summons of thunder, a king enthroned above the flood.

I hear your word in the wind.
I am your servant. I follow.
I feel the waves on my ankles.

Deep calls unto deep as your cataracts roar.
All of your breakers and billows pass over me.
I will pass through.

The rain drums. The thunder shouts.
The nuptial awns my head with jet
Of night in day.

You have posed a token upon my brow
That I may admit
No other.

Under the umbra she walks through the trough
Of the sea. Between the ramparts of surge
She feels the bottom, trudges the lowest, the deepest path.

3.

The straggly seaweed floats in the foam.
She clings to the cliff. She climbs up the rock.
She kneels on that black and craggy shore.

Who is like you? Who is like you?
Firmament's founder, fiercely I cry:
Who is like you, holy darkness?

King of the clouds, who went before her in the way,
Protecting your bride in the shadow of your hand,
Smashing the dragons' heads in the waters,

Let her not slip,
Let her not fall from the rock backwards into the deluge,
May your word like the rain not return to you empty,

Save her by water, shape the cloud
Of your glory on every place of the hill,
Lead her up the ridge, open up the sky, take her through forever.

Thunder and dove, descended now, now stay.
Lamb of passage, now reveal the sprouting olive.
Nubilous nuance of glory above me, I lift up my eyes to the mountain.

As she kneels on the shore her gaze finds the gate of the rainbow
Arching before her and over the road that ascends
The meadowy hillside where opening crocuses glow.

The Ring

1.

He stands on the land, on the mountain,
He waits in the glade, in the garden,
At noon, when the hedges are leafing, the hyacinths sweet.

Arise, make haste, my love, my beautiful one, and come,
For winter is past, the rain is over and gone,
The flowers appear in our land, the voice of the turtle is heard,

Arise and come. I have loved your eyes
As blossoms, your voice as balsam, your soul
As bride. Arise, make haste. I will be

Above you, around you, within you. My love,
Come into my garden, and know
That I am yours. Be mine

Here, on the hill of frankincense, the mountain of myrrh.
As pomegranates flourish, spikenard and saffron, calamus and
    cinnamon,
Aloes and myrrh, and the frankincense tree,

Come, my beloved, and be espoused.
The vines flower sweetly. Your eyes and your voice I desire.
Come. Come to me. Here, enclosed, is my garden. Wear my ring.

The hedges are leafing, the barberry, privet, and lilac,
Softly greening around the rubicund maple,
The coppery elm, the cherry tree's flowing pink fountain.

2.

She walks up the lawn to the psalmody throbbed by a robin
As tulips are lifting a chalice of red, then a yellow,
And hyacinths curling their incense over the earth.

Encircling rampart, rock on rock
And stone on stone, vast oaken door,
And mighty gleaming key,

Embracing forest, grove on grove
And bole on bole, high elmen arch,
And mossy glinting way,

Sheen and umbrageous garden, shade and sun,
Universe and center, yes. I am espoused
To you whose beauty makes the moons and stars

Marvel, whom lucent spirits beyond our worlds
Serve, whose earnest is this ring. The gold
Is smooth and pure and warm with noon; the band

Palpable, strange, heavy, unending; the bond,
Like you, beloved of my soul,
Unutterable.

She is with him now.
The plot is green. On the verge
A circle of fresh forsythia glistens.

3.

She kneels on the grassy earth and seems
Rooted with the grass, with the newly foliate
Hawthorns, with the penetrating beech.

Near the familiar brooks of our land
The willows hold no songless harps.
Be near me.

Beside the golden cornel, beside the daffodils,
The squills are deeper pools of blue.
Be beside me.

The tawny elm caressed by the lingering wind
Is more lissomely graced.
Be around me.

While the starry magnolia spreads radiant whiteness above,
The pastels of the hyacinths ribbon with clearer serene.
Be above me.

When the young sun rests in the early azalea,
Purple petals float alight.
Be in me.

The massive black oak is hung with gold.
The slight white birch is hung with gold.
They are together on the earth.

The Crown

1.

Yet he has left the world.
He has climbed the staircase of the air
And awaits her in the portico of the heavens.

Ascend. Forsake the earth. Relinquish
The land and the brook and the breeze
And the dandelions. Why do you stand

Looking long at the grass, looking up to the sky?
Come from the mountain, my spouse; you shall be crowned.
Come, sing the new song of the lamb,

Sing, chant, sing to him who ascended
Above the heaven of heavens to the east.
Behold his voice, his voice of strength.

Clarity is higher. Climb.
The spousal crown of the spirit,
The corona of the soul,

Will wreathe you. And do not fear
The empty steps, the spinning steeps, the stars,
The intergalactic chasms. Reach my crown.

From behind her the westering nonary sun still fingers
The buttercups, tulips, wistaria, lilacs, and dogwoods,
The chestnut torches, the luminous rubrics of the beech.

2.

*She turns from the roseate may. She abandons the last
Lavender lilacs, the dangling laburnum, the first
Fragrance of locust. Her foot tries the blue stair.*

Whom have I in heaven but you? And besides you what do I desire
On the earth though it luster pink and purple
With the beauty of the Judas tree in bloom?

Like Jacob the blessed, like John at the river,
Like Stephen the crowned, like John on the island,
I see the heavens opened and the Lord

There standing. The garden, the cities, the farmlands, the oceans,
The tops of the clouds, the air, the moon, the sun
Are below me now. Through the void I see you. I hear

A voice like a voice of many waters, like the roll
Of multiple thunders, like harpers harping with their harps.
I am here. I am there. What I desire

Now I see, what I hope now I hold.
To you whom I love wholly on earth
I am joined in heaven.

*She reaches the gleaming propylaea, the wreath above
The garland of flowering hawthorn, the circlet of cercis,
The aromatic tangle of lavender, white, and gold.*

3.

She kneels on the glittering threshold that seems a sea
Of glass, and the great colonnade seems a crystalline arbor
Wild with cascading wistaria, wondrous and weird.

Let us sing to the Lord, for his glory
Reechoes on earth and in heaven.
Grant me consonant song.

Lift up your lintels, O gates, to heaven;
Reach up, you ancient portals of song.
Admit her with the king of glory.

Holy, holy, holy, Lord; heaven
And earth are filled with the brilliant tints of your glory.
Grant her mirroring song.

You have cast out the dragon, O king of glory,
And guarded the glistening olives of song.
Admit her to the temple of heaven.

How terrible, Lord, is the glory
Of this place: the gate of heaven.
Grant me scintillant song.

It appears that beyond the gate the sign of the iris gleams
Elning from closed and open corolla below the white
Far-flung fragrance, it seems, of locust or stephanotis.

The Banquet

1.

The days since they met in the garden are seven times seven,
And tulip trees cup the sunset. He stands at the altar.
The rich virgilias drip white clusters of superabundance.

Come into my house. My hour has come
Forever. This now in flower shall fruit
Unendingly. Night shall exist no more,

For the immolation is made. The slain
Lamb is unbroken. His blood on the posts
Glows like the west. Blessed are they

Who are called to his wedding supper. This bread
Is my body. Take it and eat. And take
This cup and drink my blood. And offer

A sacrifice of praise and pay
Your vows. I espouse you to me forever
Here, where milk and honey flow

And fountains flash. If you thirst come and drink,
If you hunger eat from the tree. It is done.
I am the first and the last, the beginning and end.

From the white clouds of catalpa sweetness rises
In breeze. With a sudden sound as of wind
The sanctuary fills with the fire of evening.

2.

While a subtle quintessence of orange proceeds from the sun,
Gilding the trunks of the elms near the purpling hortensia
And purpled rose of sharon, she walks to the housel.

I magnify the Lord. With multiplied bread
You fill the hungry. I fulfill my vows
Before all in your house. I open my treasures.

Great King, yes. Today I offer the shining
Gold of possessions,
To own but you.

High God, yes. Today I offer the burning
Incense, my flesh,
To rise to you.

Beloved, yes. Today I offer the redolent
Myrrh of my soul,
To stay with you.

You have saved the good wine until now. From your mouth
I have taken honey and milk, and your blood
Has adorned my cheeks. Now dismiss me, Lord.

She has turned from life to life. The world of green
Is splashed with black, brown, yellow, red, and blue,
With nuts, with pods, with berries, drupes, and pomes.

3.

The witchhazel yellows with fall and flower. The oak is a fire.
The star that has come stands over the house. The star is a fire
That brightens as the blue roof darkens. And falling down she adores.

Stay. It is late. Stay forever.
Radiance, stay with me, drenching the root
Of my soul through the night.

Brightness, who filled your bride
With a glow like that of coals
In a paneled room, with a force

Like the thrust that rockets a chamber through the wind
And over the air to the interstellar nocturns
Chanted in limitless black beyond

Twilight, with a light
Like that of the sun naked in space,
Do not leave her ash.

It is done. And it seems like night.
But I watch through the window to the east.
It is done. And it is to be done.

Above the black-boned, white-robed tree,
Above the fireless cave of sky,
Blossoms a star, a sun.

January 6

1 p.m.

Guests crowd into the lacquered parlor.
Coconut palms converse on the shore
Above the blue lapping of the latitudinous bay.
I see this from very far away.
I am clutched within the ocean of the sun.

January 6

5 p.m.

(*Watch in a Pocket*)

Now there is nothing but dying. The choir was bright
As she knelt in her stall waiting for Vespers. The bell
Would sound in a second. She clenched the wooden side
Of the seat through the serge of long sleeves. A shift in the clef.
Now there is nothing but dying, except a life.

Part Four

The Waves Receding

Fraction

                        nothing but the nebulous
Heaven descending in mist and rain
To meet the lifting sea

Who else but he with hair of fire
Into the hollow of night

       glimmer

January 14

The traces of words do not tell
Who he is. In them is any
He. There is no other.

I will tell. He has no voice
To call with. He has no hands
That hold. He has no eyes

That burned my marrow.
The snow came again
Without footprints.

When He Went Away

Why, when he went away,
Did everything go? If the tide
Never returned, would it matter?

I sat on one of the piled orange rocks
Surveying the blue shimmer of the bay.
A cormorant kept plunging its long way across the water
While the swallows turned
And the gulls turned above.
The tide began ebbing from the black-haired rocks,
From the bronze slopes of the basin,
From the slaty floor of the harbor.
The margin of blue horizon was sinking
And people went running out among the silent heaps of fish
And the shipwrecks of the Vikings
To watch the waters vanishing over the sphere.

I sat on a rock that was becoming dusk
And remembered sunlight gleaming through the gulls' ecstatic wings,
And remembered the easy unending blue.

Vaunt

They thought there was less pain
In that love. Now that it is far away, I suppose
I will boast of the pain — of annihilation
Between white curtains, brown days
Of reexistence in noiseless passages
Peopled by solid phantoms during
Imprisonment back of the concrete walls
Of his departure, that exile of not dying,
His return like a gigantic torch that blazed
In the blackened cavern, the hard clasp
Of the candle, and then, of course,
After the mind's bright firing,
His last dissolution.

Anima

That it was a question of the soul
No one can doubt.
And that the soul like a swift
Iterates beginnings of ellipses higher
And higher over our chimneys
Also seems true.
If the soul were smoke
Would it whirl so in the air
With such winged aptitude for such celestial turns,
Would it gibber so in its ascending?

Considerations

Criticism
Limitation
Adaptation
Asseveration
Exegesis

Criticism

They wouldn't let her say
That she had a soul.
They wouldn't let her explain

What was caged behind bars
Of bones, within stones of flesh.
They didn't like the song

That her soul was singing through the chinks,
Feeling the whitest fire
Of the bluest garden.

They didn't want to hear
The loud beats of the wings of the swan
Splashing the green river of speech.

Limitation

Yet the garden, too, had a wall,
And she wanted the prairie;
She wanted, it may be said,

The harborless ocean,
The white and fathomless mountain,
The restless sky,

The vast tracts as you dart
Behind the stars,
Beyond the weathered edges

Of the endless heavens.
The wall was, it may be said,
Limit's limit.

Adaptation

She sank into sense. The shadowed, tickling
Grass was grass,
Not flesh,

The tree not yew. She liked the white stripes
Beneath the needles
Of the hemlock.

And when the feathery wings were cleaving
The breeze she was still
Below.

Asseveration

She saw or almost saw
That she could renounce her soul,
Lumbering over the lawn like a swan,

But there was more. Paddling the grass,
She could or almost, for an instant,
Could utter without pomposity,

Without the original pique
That the good had dissolved with a scream
And the true with a sigh,

Without either scream or sigh,
The word that is lighted on a northern evening in June
When the lilacs and laburnums are lighted by the rain.

Exegesis

She was afraid
Because she was laughing.
But the moorhen's lapped green feet
Did not make pentameters,
And the golden rain trees did not rain
Like tragedies

But pointed radiant fingers toward the sky,
And she did not forget
Who was not in the garden.

Was she in the garden
Perhaps because she was laughing
Or perhaps because she was afraid?

Touches

What Happened
Afterward
Anapneusis
Later
Sunday Morning

What Happened

The object was there
Like a fern-leaf beech
That was like an ocean.

The object stood beyond the moon;
She reached and touched.

The object lay beyond the sun;
Breathing was fire.

She threw out names like nets;
They floated away.

She was here,
Flapping,
Aground.

Afterward

The brilliant haws of August,
Round and red and sure,
Looked upon my barren summer soul.

The white efflorescence of May,
When May touched us in the garden,
Also had looked, and had laughed,

As, in the frolic of the pool,
Flowering under the fountain,
We saw our bright image.

Anapneusis

Sometimes
He returns
And it is sweet evening.
A breath bearing a June night
Touches your gray face
And the gray scape of the moon.
You feel the green dawning
Then.

Later

Across the wall the August haws
Beamed, content.
The iron gate was chained;

By alien ways trucks blundered
Panting over the mud;
Over the rock drills thrilled.

Even from the green and white of May
How could I touch a summer
Shut up for construction?

Sunday Morning

Wave upon wave the fern-leaf beech
Rose to the sky.
Then she would have plunged
Into the arms that were those oceanic branches
If she had not almost understood

That the tree was only an image
Of the sea,
That the sea was only a mirror
Of the sky,
That the sky was only a dream

Of the garden at the top of the fagaceous stair
Where, dancing on the azure undulation of the lawn,
She was touched by the spray of the torrential tree
Like which
Light splashes.

Recall

Affect and Effect
Sequel
Precision
Sequence
Effect and Cause

Affect and Effect

She loved her ringgiver more
Than the thegn his lord.

She loved her illuminator more
Than a bud the sun.

She looked unendingly nightward. She heard
A golden circlet clinking over stone.

Her naked finger
Felt her empty eye.

Sequel

That stony night was large:
The tree found rock at root and branch.

And we had charted the sparkling leaves
And traced the streams to their flowers.

Life had dropped into our mouths.
And now petrifaction began

As the cavern thickened.
And now our dreams were fossilized.

Precision

Did she care about the old things?
Did she hunger for the plums of the past?

Did her hand ache to curve around the smooth candle,
To feel her finger circled by the firm ring?

Did her head seem bare unveiled
And seem light uncrowned?

There was something else.
There was something infinitely else.

Sequence

When the tree of life had died
We were surprised.

Our feasting had developed into a habit.
The diminution was slow.

The scanty petals were pretty.
The final fruits were sweet.

The rock was dry and hard.
The dust was dry and soft.

Effect and Cause

All shall dawn from nothing.
That was how it was.

In the vacant night of the veil she waited
For the brilliant crown.

Dust rushed upon the bud
As the rose was opening on the stone.

However, where are the garlands of tomorrow?
Night bore night.

Consequence

Arms reach through the winter wanting
    More than a white
Robe to breast, to stem the slanting
    Persistent sleight

Of the white wind that is more than fleet.
    Pulling a gold
Gown tight in the white sheet,
    A crocus, cold,

Is not so cold as a course through the green
    And gold of the valley,
Run by one who has not foreseen
    What it is to dally.

Golden speed has sped where the crafty
    Wind can follow.
Arms reach through the winter. Daphne
    Longs for Apollo.

Narcissus

Slender bloom	bloom
Sweet sun	sun
Clear breeze	breeze
Gentle leaf	leaf
Welcome	come
Here I am	I am
I see you	you

Read the echo

Ingredients

Take wind and rain
A November evening
Friday at five
Long splashes of traffic
A gray sky glowing rose faintly
An oak with a glassy trunk
Black ferny branches waving against the great gray
The faint gray rose
That wild waving
That large sky
That beating of sky
Unrest
A memory
An old what an old stirring
God behind the oak
Glowing
God behind the solid sky

I Won't Say Yet

I won't say yet that he didn't
Press my chest and my head
From within. If he comes again
I'll ask him whether he is a fire
That alters the heart, a light
Like the scent of nectarous lindens
Filling June gardens, or whether
He isn't.

Resume

Arise, make haste, my love, he said,
    My dove, make haste and come.
For nine long years she heard him call,
    For nine years she was dumb.

The fringes of the oak were gold
    Beneath the morning's dome,
The candle of the world was bright
    When she stepped from her home.

The sonance of the ocean rose
    As she stood on the shore.
The breezes brooded on the rocks
    Above perpetual pour.

His breath was brooding in the breeze,
    His voice raced from the wave,
The candle of his countenance
    Lit all the sapphire cave.

His eyes gazed down upon the oak
    Through all the cloudy bars,
The fringes of his garment brushed
    The dandelion stars.

She saw, she walked where he had walked,
    Drew in the breath he lent,
She flamed, she broke the barrier,
    She spoke the great assent.

He set a ring upon her hand,
    A veil upon her hair.
How could she feel that the solid fact
    Was founded upon air?

The air has floated through the sky
    Above the bony tree,
The sky has fallen through the bones
    And into the swish of the sea.

The church is now a tourist spot,
    The candle packed in lace,
The veil is folded in a box,
    The ring laid in a case.

The motor of the mind runs on,
    The freeze-dried thoughts grow wet:
In every set the membership
    Includes the empty set.

Sloughing

Miles of white cloth are my wake,
And I'm still unwinding.
I'm still warm, wrapped in these bands.

I wanted to open my heart to the chill
Of myself, to know I was alone on this darkening
Ocean of rock and dust.

I wanted to feel the limits of unconnected
Self, unsnared by the sharing of endless
Shining layers of vision.

I'm still snug,
Clothed in that hot other,
Wound up in that bright Infinite.

Finding

Wanting to know the dark
Of herself, she found she was alone in a swirl
Of stars, in circles of charges.

It was not herself that she discovered
As she wandered the pocks of the moon.
It was cosmic. It was not she.

Romulus Religiosulus

He walked among imagined ills
    Singing imagined good.
Wasn't there enough that was real?
    O dizzying God.

He popped the pods of the golden rain.
    Cloudlets harried his heart,
The dark night, too. The supremely
    Attractive had hurt,

Inclined from high beyond the sky
    To greet, to shrivel, to rot.
The silvered folio flatted
    On every note.

The Persian script on the Chinese jar
    Skywrote powdered blue.
He lay on the greensward, deep in July,
    Reading by the golden rain tree.

Lemma

Subtensa evanescens anguli contactus, in curvis omnibus curvaturam finitam ad punctum contactus habentibus, est ultimo in ratione duplicata subtensae arcus contermini.

Isaac Newton.

"I am."
The book trembled. My hand
Was numb. My mind
Was burning. Time

Fell into a hole. "I am, to whom you shall be."
There was my clause. There was the least
Reason and the greatest, the first
Relation and the last. And then with a whir

That page blew over, that fire went out, and circumstance
Blocked off am and toppled shall
Into the newly fuming hell
Of the evanescent subtense.

It Was Nice

It was nice to be loved by one
Who was, however, so close that you might take him
Perhaps for granted — or was it so far?
And if he should return would I fling aside
These warm, heavy arms that never come quite that close,
This flashing mind that never goes quite that far?

Comparing

Comparing over a canyon as craggy and vast
As that on the far shore of which I sat
With my arms around my knees
And your long arms over mine

Is like comparing the sun with the grass,
The grassy stream with the willow,
The cosmic tree with this lush square yard
Where we camped on our jackets.

We

The green sea is shouting to the shore,
The purple bird is crying to the perch,
I am praying.

The gray wave strains for the land,
The black grackle strains for the seed,
I am trying.

The rasping wave slides back,
The rasping grackle flies off,
I am going.

Journal

The brine dried on their legs.
Then, through the wordless night,
He and the hound trudged up,
With the mothering ocean behind them.

Kingbold he watched the clang of dawn
Far from the sea. The slumbering dog
Did not stir.
He stirred

And saw that it was good,
And set a shade against the day,
A light against the dusk,
Explaining this and that. God

Forstood him till he shouted the noon vow,
Called the clauses of the afternoon.
But maybe in the murmur of his evensong
There was something of a recantation.

Dark-sparkling ocean, do you hold
Answers to apostrophe?
Silence rocked on the dim roll of the sea.
He did not listen in the new light.

Passage

I'll try not to pretend
To more than it was. I was struck
And shot down shadowed corridors
To that world below visited often
By famous others: Orpheus, Heracles, Theseus,
The Greek of many resources, and the pious Roman.

I forget how it was down there. I must have drunk,
Carelessly, a little Lethe there.
I must have drunk also a little Fire,
For when I returned to stare at the blue panes
Beyond the sweep and splash of sun and wind
Caught in the golden plumage of the birch,

I found that I was burning, not to return
Down there to that dim realm
But rather to quaver upward toward the opposite pole,
Sighted more sharply out of the depths,
Pulling more pungently on my bruised body,
Calling more succulently my resuscitated soul.

Shaking

If I did shake you off
Where would I be? Why do I cling
To your frail fragrant presence as one would cup
A catalpa chalice on the last day of June?
And what would happen if I could dive
Once and for all out of the tenuous nest
Where I nest in you?

Would I go on
Falling through the deep black water
Until there was only I for the moment
Before there was only the water,
Or would my frantic escaping self
Be grabbed by another
Lesser you?

Unshaken

Someone else held me,
But you didn't go away.
There was no thunderbolt,
No deluge,
No flattening,
No trickling out.
When I went back you were there,
No less dear,
And, I thought, warmer,
More comfortable.

Your Right Hand

Is it wrong to be snug
In this cozy shrine
With your warm arm around me
And your fond hand pumping my blood
While your other hand sows hurricanes?

Advent

O come. We cry. Blasts
Boom, and hearts tremble.
As the forest's limbs quiver in the north winds
Hearts tremble in David's house and ask no symbol.
At dawn white hemlock hands dissemble
The candid feathery claws of aquilonian ghosts
Under benighted skies, and pods of virgilia
Hanging hiss like fissile paramecia with winds as cilia.
Waters hang on rocks, prisoners in cells,
Frozen clothes from broken windows, dark dreams from broken bells.
Stilled are the timbrels. The crooked path ends
In slumbering tundras on shadowy lands.
Come with the south wind. Come.
Turn back, unconquered sun.
The trees will clap their hands.

O come. We cry. Boughs
Flame, and hearts fever.
There's fire in the forest, smoke in the skies,
Ash on the earth. Choking crowds crawl
From smoldering subterranean steel
Paths that pass far under the river.
Burnings in Babylon babble of Sion.
Lo, this charred cellar, the temple.
Lo, this warred wasteland, the mountain.
Cholera creeps on the edge of the desert.
Bottles beat on the base of the fountain.
Come. The lamb is thirsting with the lion.
Come. The algae thirst beside the oak.
Bedew us, skies. Clouds, rain upon the ruin.
The hills will flow with honey and with milk.

Oh come. We cry. Dikes
Drop, and hearts fail.
Lashed to palm trees through swirling nights
The strong save
Themselves. Their crops are picked and packed
By cyclone and tidal wave.
Poison flows in young urban veins,
And suburban blood
Is pumped against the snow-piled path
To the seven forty-seven. Hearts flood
And ebb. O come.
O come. What is the name?
O ark. O arc.
O moon and sun and star.
O come. O signified, save.

Today a path is pushed through the door of the sky.
Today the gates of the house of the world are raised.
Today the mellifluous heavens descend, the sun
Today as a bridegroom strides radiant from his chamber,
And Jesse's root shoots branch and bud and blossom.
Today star signals star, gift answers gift.

Today the saving lamb has come.
The bride can hear the voice of the groom.
At the voice of an angel a father was dumb.
At the greeting an infant leapt in the womb.
A tongue was loosened: The name is John.
A voice in the desert, an angel in dun,
Cried: Straighten the path that he strides upon.
Before him who stands before me I run,
Though to loosen the strap of his sandal I own
I'm unworthy. Opening skies make him known.
The voice of the father bethunders his son.
The voice of the bridegroom, his jubilant tone,
Gives joy to the friend though he stands quite alone.
The prisoner cries only: Are you the one?

The wedding guests
    Have no more wine.
But Jesus asks:
    What care of mine

Is that? My hour
    Has not yet come.
But, waiters, pour
    In pots the hum-

Drum water. Soon
    The steward tastes,
And calls the groom,
    Thinking he wastes

On drunken men
    The better wine.
Do not condemn.
    Today divine

Vintaging slakes
    Your thirst and mine,
And Jesus makes
    His nuptial sign.

O come. The sign unlocks the sky. O come.
The path is smooth and straight across the flood.
The eagle and the lightning leave the desert.
The fig tree fruits; the flight is not in winter.
O come. I rush to meet you through the night.
O come. I sit. Come striding into the silence.

The word has leapt from his sky-throne in the silence.
Good news! From the mouth of the highest, wisdom will come.
His great voice, great as a trumpet, will thunder night
Away, for great is his voice as the voice of a flood.
The hills will sing, the turtle-dove timbrel winter
Away, for the word like rain will assuage the desert.

The dew like rain has soaked into the desert,
And streams will burst forth there against the silence
Of devastation frozen into winter.
Rivers of water, wine, and milk will come
To those who thirst. Those blood-washed in the flood
Will live to watch the rainbow span the night.

The rainbow has ringed round the throne, and night
Shall be no more. A bush will burn the desert.
The bright and morning star will climb the flood.
The brightness of his rising through the silence
Will cry: A great light shall coruscant come.
A new, eternal sun will warm the winter.

The new tree that has triumphed over winter
Will pour perpetual incense through the night,
For the waste will watch the glory of Lebanon come
As Paradise bursts blooming through the desert
And wildernesses laugh above the silence
And hear the tree of life bestride the flood.

O hear the song of the lamb who has crossed the flood
And will wash the robe of his bride whiter than winter
Snow. His marriage hymn will heal the silence
Of heaven's half an hour. Throughout the night
Follow the lamb to Sion from the desert.
Amen. He is, he was, and he will come.

O come. I flood with desire the abyss of the night.
O come. I winter alone in the wind of the desert.
O come. In silence I wait. Come quickly. Come.

This Night

The rose lies long on the ribbed wet sand.
The red sun is under.

The Passover moon waits far behind thick gray folds
Of curtain. But the gray

Ocean knows — and celebrates
Untiring rite.

Dancers sway and hunch and swish and turn.
Musicians boom, clash, rasp.

Miriam sings, and death
Is drowned under foam.

Why then isn't any night
Different from any other?

Fairy Tale

She saw from her hill
At the other side of the forest
That which she desired —
Like a catalpa, but magnified, transcended,
And more than gold-and-purple-splashed white clouds
Exuding endless fragrance from the sky.

Not far into the wood she met an old woman
Of whom she did not ask the way
But who, sharp-eyed, penetrating her heart,
Said in her age-old voice: I will guide you to that
Which is, though magnified, transcended,
Like a catalpa.

And so she went with the old woman
For nine journeying years.
That they kept approaching close and closer
The scent attested. But at last
She reached the catalpa.
It was a catalpa.

My Flower

But I had   a flower
Where is   my flower
Petal   by petal
Loves me   loves me not
Loves me   loves me not
Is he   is he not
Is he   is he not
Over   and over
Over   and over
Petal   by petal

Playground

Being grown up, I don't swing any more.
I don't settle down on a splintery strip
And grip great metal-smelling chains let down from above.
I don't push off with that rapid backing up
And the sharp, hard snapping apart
Of leather and cement, and then,
With all the violence of muscle,
With all the sweet soaring of breeze,
Force my way wingward
To land only
After I have paced the sky.

Astronomia Nova

Muddy Reflection
Sidereus Nuncius
A Black Hole

Muddy Reflection

Purple burst half-furled
Out of March mud.
She forgot the straining blade
And the cloaked sod.
She forgot the blinding white
Just above musty leaves.
She forgot the chain-lines of the page
And the mirror behind the cage.

Was the moment of this bloom
An illumination
Like the golden cross and the verdant
Convolution
Of the gleaming tree of life
And its swirl of lusty leaves:
This is the beginning of the end
Of the worlds you comprehend?

The book was a flaking tome
That berated Galileo.
The mirror was a foliar blank
Where she read her ego.
The trunk of the wooden initial
Stood among trusty leaves:
There is no other world.
Purple burst half-furled.

Sidereus Nuncius

I.

A pulsar said: Among the stars
Wanders your little sun.
Upon the moon you'll all be leaping soon,
Living on Mars,
And ho! back into the sea you go.

Hey there, Fardarter!
Hey, Artemis Archer
You, bloody Wallstormer!
You there, Earthshaker!
Get below

Again and drag
The Christmas sun,
The Easter moon,
And astronomic wars
Into the primeval water,

Down with Odin to the ultimate slag.

II.

Come back, O Sun, we are cold.
Come back, O Moon, we cannot move.
Red God, while we still breathe
In the dark air, bestir us.
Lave us, Blue God, while the streams

Still run to greet you, while oaks
Root beyond rock, while dust
Still holds together. O come,
Friends, while the ice
Still breaks into purple and gold.

III.

We are gods! We can sweeten the ocean
And harness the waves.
We can harness the sun and hotly ride
By Martian mists,
Past Jupiter's clouds.

We are gods! We can race the sun
And dream of war
With Sagittarians. What to us
Are Neptune's horses
And Pluto's car?

IV.

The big ball is quieter now.
The battling ants are still.
We shall light no lights for Christmas,
And the standing sun
Is draped in our effusions.

The dark ball will roll on,
We suppose, and the plow will go
And the ocean will roll, we suppose,
And the Paschal moon
Will unveil to our candles.

V.

Thou hast conquered, O Galilean. The world's
Not our center, our rest. The spots
Flecking our sun and our eyes
Surprise
No longer.

Thou hast conquered, O Galilean. The moon
Is pocked below the virgin's feet.
Martial Rome must yield
The field
To a stronger.

Thou hast conquered, O Galilean. The earth
Shakes. The inquisitive eye
Shakes, imprisons, frees,
And sees
Through bars.

Messengers reach us from the stars.

A Black Hole

There are many stars, but my star
Has collapsed.
It is heavy on itself. An angstrom
Slice weighs tons.
No light seeps out. And nothing
Ever seeps out.
I watched that star. That star
Has sucked me in.

I watched you when you were a hot young star
Mazily aflame.
I watched you when you were a flashing giant
Heightening my sky.
I heard you when the brilliant call of the swan
Stirred my earth.
I felt you when great waves of constellations
Shook my shore.

There are many stars, but my star
Has fallen in.
It is heavy with itself. An angstrom
Scoop weighs tons.
No light comes out. And nothing
Ever can come out.
I watched that star. That star
Has sucked me up.

Commemoration

Yet
I remember
In the pomegranate garden
We met
For ever

Part Five

Difference

Sometimes It's Hard

Sometimes it's hard to believe
That it didn't happen,
That no one came through the night
Into the stone chapel, like cold
Wrapping around you, filtering through you,
But, unlike cold, warm.

Anamnestic

She was walking on the bricks of the walk
Beside the bricks of the wall
Outside the garden,

Going from here to there
Where she had gone from here to there
Nine hundred times

And back again. Those red rectangles
Do not change greatly, nor do times,
One past after another, year by year. This time

Seventeen hundred ninety-nine instants
In nine years fell away. She felt
The first time, the black serge skirt on her ankles,

The sagging black belt, black oxfords tightly laced.
Her red hem brushed her knees.
On the gray of the grass beyond the red wall a fat

February robin fed on berries red as his chest.
The witchhazel sunbeams turned to infernal gold.
Someone different walked in her shoes.

Pygmalion

You made me.
You knew me.
You came. A sun
Flamed in the room,
Drew staring eyes,
Held blinking heart,
Wrenched self from socket.
I knew you.
I made you.

The Gardens of Flora Baum

Set in 11-point Scala OT, the Open Type
version of the typeface created in
1990 by Dutch type designer
Martin Majoor and first
used for printing
programs at
Vredenburg Music
Centre, Utrecht. The name
honors Milan's La Scala opera house.

Printing: Lulu.com

Book design: Roger Sinnott